HARVEST CELEBRATIONS

Clare Chandler

The Millbrook Press
Brookfield, Connecticut

FESTIVALs

Published by The Millbrook Press
2 Old New Milford Road
Brookfield, Connecticut 06804

Editors: Sarah Doughty and Cath Senker
Designer: Tim Mayer

First published in 1997 by Wayland Publishers, Ltd.
61 Western Road, Hove, East Sussex, BN3 1JD

Library of Congress Cataloging-in-Publication Data

Chandler, Clare.
Harvest celebrations / by Clare Chandler.
p. cm
Includes bibliographical references and index.
Summary: Discusses the significance of some of the harvest
festivals around the world and describes how they are
celebrated.

ISBN 0-7613-0964-0 (lib. bdg.)
1. Harvest festival—Juvenile literature. [1. Harvest festivals.
2. Festivals.]
I. Title.
GT4380. C48 1998
394.264—dc21   97-32872
                                                 CIP
                                                  AC

Printed and bound by L.E.G.O. S.p.A., Vicenza, Italy

Picture acknowledgements
The Bridgeman Art Library 9 both; Britstock 20;
C.M Dixon 11 both; Chris Fairclough Colour
Library 4 (top left), 6 bottom, 17 top; ET Archive
14; Mary Evans 8/9, 10; Eye Ubiquitous 4 bottom
right, 13 top (Paul Seheult), 19 top; Hutchison 25,
28 bottom; Impact title page (Mark Henley), 5 top
left (Christophe Bluntzer), 7 (Mark Henley), 18
(Francesco Rizzoli), 23 (Christophe Bluntzer), 24
top (Piers Cavendish), 27 top (Piers Cavendish);
Japan National Tourist Organization 22; Christine
Osborne 17 bottom, 29; Oxford Picture Library 27
bottom; Panos 4 bottom left, 24 bottom; Tony
Stone Worldwide 5 top (David Young Wolff), 15
(David Young Wolff), 26/7 (Simon Jauncey);
Topham 5 bottom left; Trip 19 bottom, 21;
Wayland Picture Library 12, 13; Zefa 16.

Permissions
Although the publishers have attempted to
contact permission holders, we apologize if we
have been unable to contact the owners to secure
permissions.

CONTENTS

HARVEST AROUND THE WORLD

Children in schools all over Britain celebrate Harvest Festival in the autumn. They give thanks for the food they eat and bring a small gift of food for the harvest display that is later given to people in need.

A fishing festival in Nigeria, Africa. The festival lasts for two days and marks the end of the fishing season in February. The celebrations include displays of bare-hand fishing, swimming, and canoe racing.

In India, Hindus celebrate the sugarcane harvest in January. This is a time for parties and feasts that include sweet rice puddings.

A family shares a special Thanksgiving dinner in the United States. It is traditional to eat turkey as a reminder of the Pilgrim Fathers' first successful harvest in America.

The Chinese celebrate a Mid-Autumn Festival in September when they go out at night and, by the light of candles and lanterns, watch the full moon and pray for a good rice harvest.

Corn being harvested in New Zealand. As New Zealand is in the Southern Hemisphere, most crops are harvested in February and March.

A SUCCESSFUL HARVEST

Harvest is a wonderful time when farmers can see the fruits of their year's work being gathered in. When the hard work is over and the crop has been safely stored, it is time to celebrate.

Every day of the year, a harvest is being gathered somewhere in the world. Wherever there is a successful crop, people hold a festival. Festivals take place at various times of the year depending on the crop, the climate, and whether the people live in the Northern or Southern Hemisphere. For example, in New Zealand, the corn harvest takes place in February or March, while in Europe farmers harvest similar crops between August and October.

In India there are rice harvests in January, and in Europe there are wheat harvests in September and grape harvests in November. In some tropical areas, where there is plenty of rain and sunshine, fruit and vegetables can be harvested throughout the year.

Grapes are picked in the autumn to make wine and grape juices.

The birth of young farm animals is also a cause for celebration. For those who live by the sea, festivals are held at the end of the fish harvest.

Most of the major religions have at least one festival every year that is related to harvest. It is a time when people can thank their god for providing them with food. These festivals vary greatly—they all have different customs and rituals—but they all share the same ideas of celebration, giving thanks, and sharing.

THE HARVEST

The silver rain, the shining sun,
The fields where scarlet poppies run,
And all the ripples of the wheat
Are in the bread that I do eat.

So when I sit for every meal
And say a grace, I always feel
That I am eating rain and sun,
And fields where scarlet poppies run.

Alice C. Henderson

Plantains grow in very hot places. This is Tamil Nadu in southern India.

THE HISTORY OF HARVEST FESTIVALS

In the past, most people lived in small communities and produced their own food. They grew enough crops to feed themselves and their animals for the year, and relied on their livestock for basic goods such as meat, wool, and fat for making candles. If the crop failed it meant a bitterly hard year ahead, sometimes even starvation. So when the harvest was good and there was plenty for people and their animals to eat, it was a time for great celebration.

Everyone joined in for the harvest, including children. Before the nineteenth century, when machines were invented to help do the work, the crops were cut and stacked by hand—as they still are today in many poor countries. It was hard and heavy work, lasting from sunrise to sunset.

Chinese people in the nineteenth century pray to the harvest moon for a good crop.

This picture of harvesting was painted by Pieter Brueghel the Elder in the sixteenth century. The farmers are making hay in the field.

After many weeks of tiring work, when the harvest had been safely brought in, people celebrated with feasts and parties. They took part in special customs and rituals that they believed would help make the crops grow the following year.

People have been farming for thousands of years. The first people to see seeds growing into new plants could not understand what made them grow. They saw that sometimes their crops would grow strong and there would be plenty to eat and at other times the crops would fail and they would go hungry.

For hundreds of years cereal crops were cut with scythes like these; it was back-breaking work.

Ancient peoples in many parts of the world believed that a spirit lived in the crops that they grew. They thought that when the fields were harvested the spirit was losing its home and would be hiding in the last bundle of stalks that were cut. So the last sheaf was cut carefully and kept until the next harvest or plowed into the soil. In this way farmers were making sure the spirit stayed with them and gave them a good crop the following year. Sometimes the last few stalks were made into little doll-like figures, which represented the grain spirit.

Dolls like this were thought to hold the grain spirit from one harvest to the next.

HUMAN SACRIFICE

It was the custom for ancient people in many parts of the world to sacrifice human beings at harvest. This was supposed to make sure of a good crop the following year. The people of Cañar in Ecuador, South America, used to sacrifice one hundred children every year at harvest.

The ancient Greeks believed in a goddess of the harvest called Demeter. The story was that Demeter had a beautiful daughter, Persephone. One day Persephone was picking flowers in a meadow when the king of the underworld kidnapped her and took her to be his wife in Hades (the underworld). Demeter was so angry and unhappy that she said nothing should grow on earth until her daughter was returned to her. The crops all failed and there was a terrible famine until the gods came to an agreement. The king of the underworld would allow Persephone to come up to the earth for nine months of every year but the other three months she was to stay with him in Hades.

An ancient Greek painting shows the king of the underworld with his wife, Persephone.

This is how the ancient Greeks explained that there are three months of the year when nothing will grow; it is only when Persephone returns in spring that life returns to the earth.

This tomb painting from the sixth century shows the ancient Italian grain goddess Ceres with two attendants. The word cereal comes from her name.

RELIGIOUS FESTIVALS

Christian

In the Old Testament of the Bible, it says that people should set aside one tenth of their crops in order to feed widows and others who are less well off than themselves. Sharing has become an important part of Christian harvest festivals.

At the end of the harvest, Christians all over the world take gifts to their church. If they grow their own fruit and vegetables they take some of those and if not, they will take some store-bought cans or boxes of food. People often bring bunches of autumn flowers from their gardens. Sometimes loaves of bread are baked in the shape of a sheaf of grain and added to the other produce to make a beautiful, colorful display. There is a special harvest service in the church when God is thanked for providing all these good things. Afterward the food is given to people who are in need; often to the elderly or homeless.

Schools often hold their own harvest festivals. Children are encouraged to bring a gift of food from home.

In Europe Harvest Festival takes place in October. In London, the market-stall holders hold a celebration at harvest time. They are called Pearly Kings and Queens because they decorate their costumes with mother-of-pearl buttons. In countries in the Southern Hemisphere, such as Australia and New Zealand, the harvest is completed in March, so that is when they celebrate.

This beautiful loaf of bread has been baked in the shape of a sheaf of grain for the harvest display.

TITHES

For hundreds of years, up to the 1920s, farmers in Britain had to give the Church a tithe, or one tenth, of all their harvest, including animals, every year. So the parson would be given every tenth pig or lamb born and every tenth sheaf of grain was carried off to his tithe barn. This was a very unpopular payment and made many farmers bitter and angry. The farmers' feelings are expressed in the words of an old harvest song:

We've cheated the parson,
we'll cheat him again,
For why should the Vicar
have one in ten?

A Pearly Queen. The market traders of London dress in these costumes for their traditional harvest festival.

Thanksgiving

Thanksgiving in the United States is not just about thanking God for the harvest. In December 1620 a group of settlers called the Pilgrims arrived in America. They had sailed from England aboard a ship called the *Mayflower* in order to start a new life in a new country. They called the place that they found New England and they were some of the first settlers from Europe to make their homes in North America.

When the Pilgrims reached America it was too late in the year to plant seeds. Without any crops, they had very little to eat. Despite help from the local Native Americans, nearly half of them died during that first winter, mostly of starvation.

In the spring the Pilgrims planted seeds and by the end of the summer they had gathered a very good harvest. They held a great feast with the Native Americans to celebrate and to thank God. They ate geese, fish, wild turkeys, peas, and corn-rye bread.

Some Pilgrim Fathers in their plain black clothes joining the Mayflower *before it sailed for North America.*

It became a tradition to hold a Thanksgiving Day every year. On that day, American families gather together to share a special meal, usually including turkey, as a reminder of the Pilgrims' first feast. Other traditional foods are cranberry sauce, and pumpkin pie. On Thanksgiving Day, Americans today give thanks not just for the year's harvest, but to remember and thank the Native Americans for their help.

Thanksgiving Day is also celebrated in Canada, but because winter arrives there earlier than in the United States, it is held on the second Monday in October every year.

Americans celebrate Thanksgiving with a special meal that includes roast turkey.

In 1941, Thanksgiving became an official public holiday in the United States, to be celebrated on the fourth Thursday in November. That day was chosen because the Pilgrim Fathers signed the Mayflower Compact, the first plan of government for their new life, on November 21, 1620, just before they landed in America.

Jewish

The Jewish festivals of Shavuot and Sukkot are closely related to harvest. Shavuot, which takes place in May or June, was originally known as the Feast of the Harvest. It was the time when the Jewish people offered the first fruits of the field in thanks to God.

During Shavuot, homes and synagogues are decorated with flowers, and in some countries fresh grass is strewn on the floor. As well as a feast, there is singing and dancing, and harvest produce is shared. The custom is to eat dairy foods and avoid meat and fish at this time.

Synagogues are decorated for the festival of Shavuot as a reminder of the flowers that bloomed all over Mount Sinai, in Israel.

The festival of Shavuot also celebrates God giving the Torah to the prophet Moses on Mount Sinai. It is said that the Jews waited so long for Moses to return that their milk turned to cheese. That is why cheesecake and cheese-filled pancakes are traditional Shavuot foods.

Sukkot takes place in the autumn. This is a joyful festival when Jews remember the time that their people traveled from Egypt through the desert to the land of Canaan (now Israel). The festival lasts for a week and during this time families are meant to live in a sukkah, a shelter that they build to remind them of their ancestors' wanderings in the desert. They make the sukkah either inside or outside their home, or sometimes in the garden shed. It is covered with greenery and becomes a very pleasant place to eat meals and entertain friends.

These children are decorating their sukkah for the week of Sukkot.

Every day during Sukkot four plants—citron, palm, myrtle, and willow—are waved back and forth in every direction. These plants represent the harvest and the fertility of the land.

Jews in West Jerusalem buy the four plants—citron, palm, willow, and myrtle—that they will hold during the synagogue services in Sukkot.

Hindu

Hindu festivals are celebrated in various ways in different parts of India. All over the country, Hindus celebrate the sugarcane harvest in January. In the south the festival is called Pongal and lasts for two or three days. The word Pongal means "to boil" and the festival is named after the custom of eating rice boiled with sugar. The sugarcane is crushed and boiled to make a sugary syrup called jaggery. This is added to boiled milk and rice to make a pudding. After it is offered to the gods, a great feast is held and the pudding is eaten along with other delicacies. The second day of the festival is devoted to the sun god, Surya, and the rice pudding is offered to the sun.

In January Hindus in northern India celebrate Lohri. This is a joyful festival when families and friends visit the homes of children who were born in the past year. They gather around bonfires in the cold winter air, sing songs together, and share meals that also include rice cooked in sugarcane syrup.

CATTLE PONGAL

The third day of Pongal is a special day devoted to cattle, which are sacred to Hindus. Each family chooses a cow, which they feed on boiled rice, worship, and then drive away. All the cattle are decorated with garlands of flowers and rice sheaves, and their horns are painted. The cattle are then herded together and driven off by the sound of drumming and of a large wind instrument like an oboe.

Women in southern India decorate the ground for the festival of Pongal.

One of the most spectacular Hindu festivals is Onam, which takes place in Kerala on the south-western tip of India. It is a celebration of the harvest at the end of the rainy season, in August or September. People decorate their homes, wear new clothes, and give each other presents. Children weave mats out of flowers they have gathered from the fields. After they have been to the temple to give thanks for the harvest, they hold a wonderful feast of spicy rice, vegetables, and sweet puddings.

Snake-boat races like this are held in the state of Kerala to celebrate the festival of Onam.

This is followed by snake-boat races that take place in the lagoons along the shore. Huge boats carved to represent animals and covered with green and red umbrellas are rowed by hundreds of oarsmen.

Sikh

Sikhs hold a festival in April, just before the first grain crop is harvested in India. This festival is called Baisakhi and it is the beginning of the Sikh religious year.

During the festival Sikh's get together and play games, organize races, buy and sell animals, and listen to speeches about the gurus, the Sikh religious teachers. One of the features of the festival is spectacular dancing performed by troops of men. Only when the festival is over do farmers begin the work of harvesting the grain crop.

Sikhs at a fair. The most visible signs of their faith are that their hair and beards are uncut and they wear turbans.

Offerings of fruit and nuts are displayed at the Zoroastrian festival of Mihr Jashan.

Zoroastrian

Zoroastrianism is one of the oldest religions in the world. It was founded by the Persian prophet, Zarathushtra, over five hundred years before Christ lived. Zoroastrians do not have a weekly holy day, like a Sunday or Sabbath, but instead have holy days and festivals throughout the year.

In October, Zoroastrians, who live mainly in Iran and northern India, hold a harvest festival called Mihr Jashan. It lasts for five days and during this time they enjoy feasts and parties, and farmers take offerings of crops such as wheat and cotton to their temple.

OTHER HARVEST FESTIVALS

Japan

In Japan, rice is the staple crop and it is eaten with every meal. The Japanese hold several festivals that are linked with the rice harvest. In the spring, there is a special ceremony in which the Japanese emperor plants the first new rice. Later in the year, in August, there is the Lantern Festival in northern Japan, to celebrate the ripening of the rice crop.

At Moon Viewing in September, people drink rice wine while looking at the beautiful full moon. They sing songs and pray for a good rice harvest. It is said that people can see the shadows on the moon of a rabbit making rice cakes.

The Lantern Festival in Japan. Each lantern represents a grain of rice.

In November, when the rice is harvested, there is the New Taste Festival. Nowadays it is a national holiday known as Labor Thanksgiving Day and is the day when the Japanese celebrate the success of their industries as well as the harvest. The festival is still celebrated by dancing and a wonderful feast at which lots of rice wine is drunk.

China

The Chinese hold a festival in September called the Mid-Autumn Festival, when they watch the full moon and pray for a good rice harvest. Moon cakes are offered to the moon. These are special cakes made of a pastry crust filled with a mixture of ground lotus fruit and sesame seeds or dates. On the top is usually a picture of the moon or the rabbit in the moon.

Children in Hong Kong are allowed to stay up late to watch the moon at the Mid-Autumn Festival.

In the Chinese districts of cities all over the world, streets are decorated and shops sell brightly colored lanterns as well as moon cakes. Children stay up late with their parents to watch the moon by the light of their lanterns and eat their cakes.

Africa

Africa is made up of many countries with different climates. Some countries are mountainous while others are flat, some are largely desert while others have great lakes and tropical rain forests. Therefore a wide variety of crops are grown. Corn, cassava, plantain, beans, and okra are all staple foods, and Africans have many rituals and festivals surrounding the harvesting and planting of their crops.

Some Christians set aside land in their village that they call "God's Acre." They sell the crops that they grow there at their harvest festival and give the money to the church or to people in need.

Wheat being harvested in Kenya, one of the most fertile countries in Africa.

The fishing festival at Argungu in Nigeria. The people catch the fish with nets and large gourds called calabashes.

Yams, collected ready for the Yam Harvest Festival in Ghana.

Although many Africans celebrate a Christian Harvest Festival at the same time as it is held in Europe, they also continue to hold traditional festivals that are linked with their particular crops. For example, early in September, the Ashanti people of Ghana hold a Yam Festival. This is an important harvest celebration—feasts of yams are eaten and there is drumming and dancing. It is a time when young women step into adult society and weddings often take place.

One of the most spectacular African festivals is held every year in Nigeria and marks the start of the fishing season in February. Thousands of men and boys wade into the river with large nets and drive the fish into the shallow water where they can be easily caught. The festival lasts for two days and during that time there are displays of fishing, swimming, and canoe racing.

KWANZA

Kwanza is a recent festival but one that already has some attractive family traditions. Kwanza means "first fruits" and it is a celebration by African Americans of the year's harvest in Africa. It was started in 1966 in the U.S. as a way for people to remember their African ancestors and way of life. Kwanza is held at the end of December and lasts for seven days. Each day a black, green, or red candle is lit. At the end of the week a feast is held and people give each other presents.

THE CHANGING HARVEST

Most people no longer have much to do with the production of the food that they eat. They buy everything they need from stores and, if they live in towns and cities, they rarely see the crops growing.

In the past it would have taken hundreds of people to harvest these fields. Nowadays, using these combine harvesters, the work can be done by just a few.

Farming has changed greatly in most parts of the world. The use of machinery means that fewer people are needed to work on the land and new technology has made it possible to produce food all year round.

The food in stores is often frozen, or packaged in cartons and cans. This means it will last a long time, so it can be transported and stored easily. A kitchen cabinet will often hold food from all over the world: for example, tea from India, canned tomatoes from Italy, coffee from South America, and fresh fruit and vegetables from Australia and South Africa. If one country's harvest fails, food can be bought from another country.

Right: Pineapples are put into cans at a factory in Africa. Fruit will keep for years in a can and may be exported all over the world.

Despite all this, harvest festivals remain popular, even for people who live in towns and cities where they do not see crops being planted and harvested. Harvest is a time when we can remember how precious our food is. It is also a time to give thanks for such fruitful earth, and to thank all the people who are involved in bringing food to our tables. And, if possible, it is a time to share what we have with those whose needs may be greater than our own.

Most people these days buy their food from stores and have no part in growing or producing it.

27

CALENDAR OF HARVEST FESTIVALS

Pongal, January.

During this southern Indian festival, which lasts for two or three days, Hindus celebrate the sugarcane harvest. On the third day Cattle Pongal is celebrated. The cattle are decorated and then driven off to the sound of drumming and music.

Lohri, January.

This is a northern Indian festival to celebrate the birth of children born in the past year. People gather around a bonfire and share meals that include rice cooked in sugarcane syrup.

Fishing festival, February.

The fishing festival is held every year in Nigeria to mark the beginning of the fishing season. It lasts two days. Men and boys use large nets to drive the fish into shallow water, and there are displays of fishing, swimming, and canoe racing.

Baisakhi, April 13-14.

Baisakhi is a Sikh festival celebrated just before the harvesting of the first grain crop, and it marks the beginning of the Sikh religious year. Sikhs gather together to play games and listen to speeches about the Sikh religious leaders.

Shavuot, May/June.

The Jewish festival of Shavuot was at first a harvest celebration, although it also celebrates God giving the Torah to the prophet Moses. During the festival there is singing and dancing, and harvest produce is shared.

Lantern Festival, August 5-7.

This northern Japanese festival celebrates the ripening of the rice crop. Men carry bamboo frames with glowing lanterns on them that represent ears of rice and their grains.

Onam, August/September.

This festival takes place in Kerala in southern India. People decorate their homes and give each other presents to celebrate the harvest and the end of the rainy season. A feast is held and there are snake-boat races.

Yam Festival, September.

The yam festival held by the Ashanti people of Ghana is a harvest celebration. Yams are eaten and there is drumming and dancing.

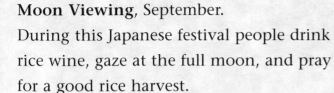

Moon Viewing, September.
During this Japanese festival people drink rice wine, gaze at the full moon, and pray for a good rice harvest.

Mid-Autumn Festival, September.
This Chinese festival is similar to the moon viewing festival in Japan. People watch the full moon and pray for a good rice harvest. Special moon cakes are offered to the moon and then eaten.

Sukkot, September/October.
During Sukkot, which lasts for a week, Jewish people remember when their ancestors traveled from Egypt to Canaan (now Israel). Every day four symbolic plants are waved to and fro to represent the harvest and the fertility of the land.

Mihr Jashan, October.
Mihr Jashan is a harvest festival held by Zoroastrians in Iran and northern India. For five days people enjoy feasts and farmers take offerings of crops to their temple.

Harvest Festival, October in Europe, March in Australia and New Zealand.
At the end of the harvest Christians take gifts to their church. There is a special harvest service in the church and then the harvest goods are given to people in need.

Thanksgiving, the second Monday in October in Canada; the fourth Thursday in November in the United States.
The Thanksgiving festival celebrates the first Thanksgiving held by the Pilgrim Fathers, settlers who arrived in America in 1620. American families prepare a special meal, often including turkey and pumpkin pie.

Labor Thanksgiving Day, November 23.
This is a national holiday when the Japanese celebrate the success of their industries as well as the rice harvest. There is a feast where rice wine is drunk, and there is dancing.

Kwanza, December 26 to January 1.
Kwanza is a celebration by African Americans in the United States of the year's harvest in Africa. It lasts for seven days and on each day a black, green, or red candle is lit. There is a feast at the end of the week.

GLOSSARY

Ancestors The people in your family who lived before you: your parents, grandparents, great-grandparents, and so on.

Famine A great shortage of food.

Immigrants People who settle in another country.

Lagoon An area of water, cut off from the open sea.

Livestock Cattle, horses, chickens, and other animals usually kept on farms.

Northern Hemisphere The half of the world above the Equator.

Parson In history, a parish priest of the Church of England who was allowed to take tithes from farmers.

Prophet A person who announces messages from God.

Rituals Formal or religious acts.

Sacrifice When a person or animal is killed to please a god.

Sheaf (plural: sheaves) A bundle of grain that has just been harvested.

Sikhism A religion that was founded in northern India in the sixteenth century and teaches that there is one God. Sikhism now has many followers worldwide.

Southern Hemisphere The half of the world below the Equator.

Staple The main food in people's diet.

Synagogue A building where Jews pray and learn about their religion.

Torah The teachings of the Jewish faith.

Tropical areas The areas of the Earth's surface on either side of the Equator between the Tropic of Cancer and the Tropic of Capricorn.

Yams Large vegetables like sweet potatoes.

OTHER BOOKS ABOUT HARVEST CELEBRATIONS

Bauer, Caroline Feller, Nadine Bernard Westcott (Illustator). *Thanksgiving Stories and Poems.* New York: HarperCollins, 1994.

Bragg, Bea, Antonia Castro (Illustrator). *The Very First Thanksgiving: Pioneers on the Rio Grande.* Boulder, CO: Harbinger Hse, 1989.

Child, Lydia Maria, Christopher North (Illustrator). *Over the River and Through the Wood.* New York: North-South Bks, 1993.

Johnson, James W., et al. *Nguzo Saba and the Festival of First Fruits: A Guide for Promoting Family and Community Values and the Celebration of Kwanzaa.* New York: Gumbs & Thomas, 1995.

Kalman, Bobbie, et al. *We Celebrate the Harvest (The Holidays & Festivals Series).* New York: Crabtree Pub, 1986.

Penner, Lucille Recht. *Eating the Plates: A Pilgrim Book of Food and Manners.* New York: Scholastic Inc, 1991.

Pennington, Dan, Don Stewart (Illustrator). *Itse Selu: Cherokee Harvest Festival.* Watertown, MA: Charlesbridge Pub, 1994.

San Souci, Robert. *N.C. Wyeth's Pilgrims.* San Francisco: Chronicle Bks, 1991.

Whitlock, Ralph. *Thanksgiving and Harvest (Holidays and Festivals).* Vero Beach, FL: Rourke Book Co, 1987.

FOR MORE INFORMATION

Henrico Recreation and Parks - Harvest Festival Posters. *http://www.co.henrico.va.us/rec/* Exchange-Harvest Festival (Korea). *http://pc159.lang.uiuc.edu/exchange/contributions/culture/festivals/KoreanHarvest.html*

"A Page from the KIDPROJ Multi-Cultural Calendar Pongaal-Harvest Festival - Singapore by Tammy and Kenneth Routh." *http://www.kidlink.org/KIDPROJ/MCC/1.14.1.html*

Songs for Thanksgiving *http://www.night.net/thanksgiving/ksongs11.html*

Links to Thanksgiving Web Sites. *http://www.webreview.com/96/11/22/hour/index.html*

Thanksgiving Games & Activities *http://www.erols.com/ouremail/Thanksgiving/GamesandAct.htm*

Tobago's Harvest Festival *http://www.tidco.co.tt/local/THF-1996/harvest/index.html*

The Festival of Onam *http://www. indiaedition.com/crosslinks/september97/onam.htm.*

INDEX